Greater Than a Tourist Book Series
Reviews from Readers

I think the series is wonderful and beneficial for tourists to get information before visiting the city.

-Seckin Zumbul, Izmir Turkey

I am a world traveler who has read many trip guides but this one really made a difference for me. I would call it a heartfelt creation of a local guide expert instead of just a guide.

-Susy, Isla Holbox, Mexico

New to the area like me, this is a must have!

-Joe, Bloomington, USA

This is a good series that gets down to it when looking for things to do at your destination without having to read a novel for just a few ideas.

-Rachel, Monterey, USA

Good information to have to plan my trip to this destination.

-Pennie Farrell, Mexico

Great ideas for a port day.

-Mary Martin USA

Aptly titled, you won't just be a tourist after reading this book. You'll be greater than a tourist!

-Alan Warner, Grand Rapids, USA

Even though I only have three days to spend in San Miguel in an upcoming visit, I will use the author's suggestions to guide some of my time there. An easy read - with chapters named to guide me in directions I want to go.

-Robert Catapano, USA

Great insights from a local perspective! Useful information and a very good value!

-Sarah, USA

This series provides an in-depth experience through the eyes of a local. Reading these series will help you to travel the city in with confidence and it'll make your journey a unique one.

-Andrew Teoh, Ipoh, Malaysia

\>TOURIST

GREATER THAN A TOURIST- DENVER COLORADO USA

50 Travel Tips from a Local

Megan M. Perry

Greater Than a Tourist- Denver Colorado USA Copyright © 2018 by CZYK Publishing LLC. All Rights Reserved.

All rights reserved. No part of this book may be reproduced in any form or by any electronic or mechanical means including information storage and retrieval systems, without permission in writing from the author. The only exception is by a reviewer, who may quote short excerpts in a review.

The statements in this book are of the authors and may not be the views of CZYK Publishing or Greater Than a Tourist.

Cover designed by: Ivana Stamenkovic
Cover Image: https://pixabay.com/en/denver-colorado-mountains-city-2228783/

Edited by:

CZYK Publishing Since 2011.

Greater Than a Tourist
Visit our website at www.GreaterThanaTourist.com

Lock Haven, PA
All rights reserved.
ISBN: 9781790770908

>TOURIST

50 TRAVEL TIPS FROM A LOCAL

BOOK DESCRIPTION

Are you excited about planning your next trip?

Do you want to try something new?

Would you like some guidance from a local?

If you answered yes to any of these questions, then this Greater Than a Tourist book is for you.

Greater Than a Tourist - Denver, Colorado USA by Megan M. Perry offers the inside scoop on Denver. Most travel books tell you how to travel like a tourist. Although there is nothing wrong with that, as part of the Greater Than a Tourist series, this book will give you travel tips from someone who has lived at your next travel destination.

In these pages, you will discover advice that will help you throughout your stay. This book will not tell you exact addresses or store hours but instead will give you excitement and knowledge from a local that you may not find in other smaller print travel books.

Travel like a local. Slow down, stay in one place, and get to know the people and the culture. By the time you finish this book, you will be eager and prepared to travel to your next destination.

>TOURIST

TABLE OF CONTENTS

BOOK DESCRIPTION
TABLE OF CONTENTS
DEDICATION
ABOUT THE AUTHOR
HOW TO USE THIS BOOK
FROM THE PUBLISHER
OUR STORY
WELCOME TO
> TOURIST
INTRODUCTION
1. Best Times to Visit
2. Travel from the Airport
3. Places to Stay
4. Watch What You Drink
5. From LoDo to FoCo, All the Slang You Need to Know
6. Take a Bike Ride
7. Ski Down a Slope
8. Rocky Mountain High
9. Summit a 14er
10. Continental Divide
11. Experience Red Rocks
12. Experience America's Best Water Park
13. Visit Colorado's Most Exciting Restaurant

14. Experience Native American Food
15. Weigh In On the Green Chili Debate
16. Eat a VooDoo Doll Doughnut
17. Get a Drink at a Craft Brewery
18. Hit Snooze
19. Behind the Freezer Door
20. Little Man Ice Cream
21. Put your vote in for the Best Burrito
22. Burrito Pizza?
23. Rocky Mountain Oysters
24. Fool's Gold
25. Visit the Original Chipotle Location
26. Shark Yoga
27. Dancing and Bull Riding
28. The Music Scene
29. Discover the Hidden Elves
30. Ride a Rollercoaster
31. Shop Local
32. Watch How Homemade Candy is Made
33. Take Time for a Picnic
34. Big Blue Bear
35. Observe the Art Scene
36. Discover How Tea is Made
37. Catch a Top-Notch Performance
38. Chalk Art Festival
39. Denver Botanic Gardens

>TOURIST

40. The Unsinkable Molly Brown
41. Sports
42. National Western Stock Show
43. Colorado Cannabis
44. Great American Beer Festival
45. Coors Brewery
46. The Mile High City
47. Stroll Down Historical Larimer Square
48. Shop 16th Street Mall
49. Find Out How Money is Made
50. Get a Glimpse of Blucifer

TOP REASONS TO BOOK THIS TRIP

50 THINGS TO KNOW ABOUT PACKING LIGHT FOR TRAVEL

Packing and Planning Tips

Travel Questions

Travel Bucket List

NOTES

>TOURIST

DEDICATION

To my mother, Tamma, for passing on her love of Colorado and the outdoors.

To my father, Daniel, for making me believe that I can do anything that I set my mind to.

To Emmy, my dog, for always being a light in my life.

And to my husband, Cameron, for inspiring me to pursue my passions and follow my dreams.

To our dear Canadian friends,

If you ever travel to Denver, I hope this is helpful.

Love, Megan

ABOUT THE AUTHOR

Growing up in Colorado, Megan loves spending time in the outdoors. With a mother who took her hiking and father who took fishing, she grew up loving the Colorado Mountains. She has visited many sites and experienced a lot of what Denver has to offer. She loves baking, hiking, and traveling. Her love of travel inspired her to travel to many different countries in the world. While there are many amazing places in the world, none of them quite compare to Colorful Colorado.

>TOURIST

HOW TO USE THIS BOOK

The Greater Than a Tourist book series was written by someone who has lived in an area for over three months. The goal of this book is to help travelers either dream or experience different locations by providing opinions from a local. The author has made suggestions based on their own experiences. Please do your own research before traveling to the area in case the suggested places are unavailable.

Travel Advisories: As a first step in planning any trip abroad, check the Travel Advisories for your intended destination.
https://travel.state.gov/content/travel/en/traveladvisories/traveladvisories.html

FROM THE PUBLISHER

Traveling can be one of the most important parts of a person's life. The anticipation and memories that you have are some of the best. As a publisher of the Greater Than a Tourist book series, as well as the popular 50 Things to Know book series, we strive to help you learn about new places, spark your imagination, and inspire you. Wherever you are and whatever you do I wish you safe, fun, and inspiring travel.

Lisa Rusczyk Ed. D.
CZYK Publishing

OUR STORY

Traveling is a passion of the "Greater than a Tourist" series creator. Lisa studied abroad in college, and for their honeymoon Lisa and her husband toured Europe. During her travels to Malta, an older man tried to give her some advice based on his own experience living on the island since he was a young boy. She was not sure if she should talk to the stranger but was interested in his advice. When traveling to some places she was wary to talk to locals because she was afraid that they weren't being genuine. Through her travels, Lisa learned how much locals had to share with tourists. Lisa created the "Greater Than a Tourist" book series to help connect people with locals. A topic that locals are very passionate about sharing.

>TOURIST

WELCOME TO
> TOURIST

INTRODUCTION

"Because in the end, you won't remember the time you spent working in the office or mowing your lawn."

– Jack Kerouac

We rarely hear someone talk about the amazing day they had when they woke up, ate, went to work, came home, watched a movie, then went to bed. Those days are forgettable because they are routine. Traveling is so important because it gets you out of your routine to experience something new. Being in a new city gives you opportunities unique to where you are.

This edition of Greater Than a Tourist will give you tips from a Denver local. Nicknamed Colorful Colorado, Colorado is home to a vast mountain region and wildlife as well as a flourishing city life. Nestled in the middle of the state is its capital, Denver. Denver is a hub for delicious food, interesting history, and unique things to do. The city offers something for everyone from outdoor adventures to exploring history to getting a great bite to eat.

>TOURIST

1.BEST TIMES TO VISIT

Denver is a beautiful city to visit any time of the year, so the best time to visit depends on what you are visiting for. Spring is a great time to visit to score hotel deals and beat the crowds, but you will probably experience rainy and sometimes snowy weather. If you come to hike, the spring is beautiful with a variety of wildflowers blooming. Summer is the most popular time to visit. The weather is sunny and warm making it a perfect time to be outdoors. There are a wide variety of festivals going on in the summer, making Denver a busy city all summer long. Fall is when most of the culinary festivals take place, including The Great American Beer Fest and A Taste of Colorado. This is also a great time to hike or drive through the mountains to see the leaves changing colors. With so much going on, fall is also a very popular time for tourists to come. Winter typically attracts tourists coming for winter sports creating heavy traffic. No matter when you visit, be prepared for the weather to change quickly.

2. TRAVEL FROM THE AIRPORT

There are a lot of options to get to downtown Denver from the airport. I would recommend renting a car to save time as downtown Denver is about a 30-minute drive from the airport. Renting a car will also give you the flexibility to take a day trip to the mountains. If you can't or don't want to rent a car, you can get to Denver by rail, taxi, or a rideshare app like Uber or Lyft.

If you are traveling by rail, Line A will take you directly from the airport to Union Station. Union Station is very central to the rest of downtown. To take the rail, just follow the signs to the platform. You can purchase tickets here and catch the rail which runs every 15-30 minutes. The rail has luggage storage and is wheelchair accessible as well. Taking just over 35 minutes to get to Denver, it is a great option to get downtown.

Traveling by taxi, Uber, or Lyft are also great options. The airport has signs pointing you to the pickup locations of taxis and rideshares. Keep in mind that if you are taking a taxi, Uber, or Lyft there is an additional airport access fee added to each trip.

>TOURIST

3. PLACES TO STAY

Denver has a wide variety of places to stay ranging widely in price and quality. When looking for a place to stay, be sure to check out Airbnb as there are a lot of quality options in Denver. But if you prefer a hotel, there are a few unique hotels that stand out. The Warwick Denver Hotel has one of Denver's only rooftop pools. From the pool, you have an amazing view of the city. The Curtis Hotel is a pop culture-themed hotel with modern and stylish rooms. The Maven hotel has modern rooms with an amazing lobby and common spaces. The hotel features more than 400 pieces of art. If you have an early departure, a late arrival, or you have an overnight layover; consider staying at the Denver Airport Westin Hotel which is connected to the airport, so you won't have to travel far.

4. WATCH WHAT YOU DRINK

If you are coming from a place close to sea level, you may feel some mild effects from the elevation gain. The air is thinner and dryer up here, but don't let it scare you, if you keep these few things in the back of your head, you'll be fine.

Make sure to watch what you drink. Drinking water will help your body adjust to the altitude. Staying hydrated is one of the most important things that you can do. Also, keep in mind that alcohol will affect you differently than at sea level, so go a little easy on the alcohol. In addition to watching what you drink, watch your physical activity. There is less oxygen available at higher elevations making exercise more difficult on your body. If you typically go for 5 mile runs in the morning, try going for a 3-mile run instead.

5. FROM LODO TO FOCO, ALL THE SLANG YOU NEED TO KNOW

Colorado has a number of colloquialisms. The first has to do with the abbreviations of city or area names. If you hear someone refer to being from The Springs, or if you're told you should go to The Springs, they are referring to Colorado Springs. While there are many popular "springs" cities in Colorado, like Glenwood, Steamboat, or Pagosa, "The Springs" always refers to Colorado Springs. Some other common terms are any of the "o" names like LoDo

>TOURIST

(lower downtown), NoCo (Northern Colorado), RiNo (River North Arts District), or FoCo (Fort Collins).

The second has to do with number references. These are the most prominent number references you'll see in Denver: 5280, 303, and 420. 5280 (fifty-two eighty) is referring to Denver as the mile-high city since there are 5,280 feet in a mile. 303 (three o three) is Denver's area code, you'll see this number on things ranging from shops to food to the band 3OH!3. 420 (four-twenty) refers to April 20th or weed day. While there is debate as to how this day was chosen, everyone is in agreement of the meaning of 420.

The third has to do with directions. Growing up in Denver, it was appropriate to give directions using the mountains as a reference. You might ask someone for directions and they will tell you to head towards the mountains (west) or away from the mountains (east).

6. TAKE A BIKE RIDE

Like many other big cities, Denver has a bike rental program. The rental program has rental options by the hour, day, week, and more. There are over 80 stations to check out and return bikes in Denver. Denver has a vast system of bike lanes connecting the city's parks and attractions. One of my favorite places to bike is Confluence Park. It has a wide variety of paths and benches to take a break. If you are looking for something more exciting, you can bike to Confluence Park and then rent a kayak and go down the river close by.

7. SKI DOWN A SLOPE

Colorado has a lot of amazing ski resorts. During the winter, there are buses that will take visitors directly from the airport to many of Colorado's ski resorts. Out of the ski resorts close to Denver, two stand out from the rest: Keystone and Loveland. Keystone is overall an amazing ski resort. It is known for its size, quality of runs, and number of lifts. For those that want to get a little more adventurous, Keystone also has terrain parks. It has cute shops and cafes to warm up with coffee and hot chocolate, giving you the classic ski town vibe. If you are looking to spend multiple days skiing, there are a number of places you can stay right in Keystone.

> TOURIST

Keystone is about an hour and a half away from Denver while Loveland is about an hour away. But with so many people driving to the resorts, traffic can get backed up, especially on the weekends.

Loveland is a great ski resort for beginners. It is also where I learned to ski. Loveland has one of the best bunny hills to learn on. It also has full length runs that are great for beginners. As a smaller resort, it is also easier to navigate. Because it is smaller, it is less expensive than most other resorts.

If you do not have your own skiing or snowboarding equipment, most ski resorts have their own rental facilities as well as sporting goods stores throughout Colorado. As a general rule, the closer the rental store is to the mountains, the more expensive the rental will be. All of the ski resorts offer ski and snowboard lessons for those who are just beginning, need to brush up on their skills, or want to learn more.

8. ROCKY MOUNTAIN HIGH

Denver itself is not situated in the mountains, but the mountains are close by. There are three main places to go to get to the mountains and hike: Rocky Mountain National Park, Chautauqua Park in Boulder, and Golden Gate Canyon State Park.

Rocky Mountain National Park is about an hour and a half drive from Denver. Right outside of Rocky Mountain National Park is Estes Park. Estes Park is the perfect mountain town. It is full of family-run restaurants, delicious dessert shops, and local shopping. Be sure to check out the shops on the Eastern side as they typically have the best prices.

Once you get into Rocky Mountain National Park, you can choose to either drive a scenic road or get out and hike. If you choose to drive, drive Trail Ridge Road. It offers amazing views and takes you over the Continental Divide. If you are wanting to hike, the most popular hike is Bear Lake. You can park at the Bear Lake trailhead or if the parking lot is full, take a free shuttle up to Bear Lake. The trail is family friendly and flat, so it is a good way for anyone to get out into nature. While this is the most popular hike,

>TOURIST

I'd recommend skipping it. There are a lot better, less crowded lake just a little further on.

If you are looking to do a day hike, I'd recommend hiking to Sky Pond. On the hike, you'll pass Alberta Falls, The Loch, Timberline Falls, and Lake of Glass. The hike to sky pond has so much packed in. The hike takes you through a variety of dense woods and mountain valleys. It is not uncommon to see a variety of wildlife including deer, marmots, and pika on the hike. Whether you are looking for a drive, a picturesque walk, or a straining hike, there is something for everyone in Rocky Mountain National Park.

Chautauqua Park is about a 35-minute drive from Denver. It is right in Boulder, where there are a lot of restaurants, shopping, and other things to do. If you only have a few hours to hike, hike the Flatirons. It is the most iconic hike in Boulder. The trail will get you up close to the flats where you can get an amazing view of Boulder, as well as watch rock climbers climb the flats. Make sure to arrive early as the parking lots fill up fast during the summer months.

Golden Gate Canyon State Park is about 50 minutes from Denver. It offers a variety of hikes throughout the park. If you are traveling with dogs, Golden is probably your best bet as it has one of the friendliest dog policies. One of my favorite, family-friendly trails is Raccoon Loop Trail. The 2.5-mile trail is short, relatively easy, and has a variety of scenery. If you have time while you're in Denver, don't miss out on experiencing Colorado's amazing mountains.

"Climb the mountain not to plant your flag, but to embrace the challenge, enjoy the air and behold the view. Climb it so you can see the world, not so the world can see you." -David McCullough Jr.

9. SUMMIT A 14ER

If you're not familiar with the term, a 14er is simply a mountain that is over 14,000 feet. There are 96 fourteeners in the United States. Of these 96 fourteeners, 53 of them are in Colorado. The other fourteeners are in Alaska (29), California (12), and Washington (2). Having more than half of the United States' 14ers, Colorado has become known for them.

>TOURIST

While no hike up a mountain is easy, the 14ers range in mileage and difficulty making some of them a doable task for almost anyone. Denver is in the perfect location giving you easy access to 6 fourteeners in the Front Range: Mount Evans, Pikes Peak, Longs Peak, Mount Bierstadt, Grays Peak, and Torreys Peak.

Mount Evans is one of the most popular 14ers in Colorado because of its accessibility. It is about an hour and a half drive from Denver. Mount Evans is unique because it is one of the two 14ers you can drive up (the other is Pikes Peak). It also holds the title of the tallest road in the US at 14,120 feet. You can start your hike to the peak in a variety of places depending on how long and difficult you want your hike to be. The shortest and easiest way to summit Mount Evans is to drive to the top the winding road. If you decide to drive up, you will still have to walk about a fourth of a mile from the parking lot in order to reach the summit. Like many Coloradans, this was my first 14er to summit.

Longs Peak is one of the most difficult 14ers at 14.5 miles round trip. It has higher exposure and more scrambling than any of the other 14ers in the

Front Range. The Front Range also has some of the easiest 14ers. Mount Bierstadt is one of the easiest to hike up at 5-7 miles round trip. If you are looking to summit two 14ers in a day, the Front Range has two sets you can easily do. Mount Bierstadt and Mount Evans have a route that is just over 10 miles to get both in. Grays and Torreys also have a route that is 8.5 miles round trip to summit both.

Don't let the mileage fool you. Hiking is very different than walking or hiking a flat trail. The elevation gained on a 14er is often a lot more than you would experience on a regular hike. Be aware of the trail conditions, take the right equipment, and read a trail guide before you hike one of our mountains.

If you decide to summit a 14er, stop by any Which Wich location and pick up one of their kraft paper sandwich bags. Take a picture of yourself holding the bag on any 14er in Colorado, print it out, and bring it to the shop to receive a free sandwich. Your picture along with which fourteener you hiked will be posted on their wall along with others.

>TOURIST

10. CONTINENTAL DIVIDE

The Continental Divide, or The Great Divide, separates water drainage in America. Everything east of the divide runs to the Atlantic Ocean and everything west of the divide runs to the Pacific Ocean. While there are other divides, this is the biggest and most prominent divide in North America.

There are many ways to experience The Great Divide but all require a drive west of Denver. One of the most significant ways is to hike it. The Continental Divide trail runs from the border of Mexico up to Canada. This is one of the three prominent Mexico to Canada trails. Few people ever fully hike one, let alone all three. If you do hike all three, you hold the title of the triple crown. Most people don't have the time or desire to hike the full Continental Divide, but you can still see it. A great way to experience it is driving across The Continental Divide on Trail Ridge Road in Rocky Mountain National Park or Loveland Pass just off of I-70.

11. EXPERIENCE RED ROCKS

The Amphitheater at Red Rocks is more than just a cool place to watch a concert. It is the only naturally occurring, perfect acoustic amphitheater in the world. Since 1941, musicians of all levels have played at Red Rocks. In addition to concerts, you can also enjoy movies, workouts, shopping, biking, and dining. If you are visiting Colorado during the summer, be sure to catch a movie at Red Rocks. Before your event, stop by the visitor's center where you can watch a short film about the geology and history of Red Rocks.

12. EXPERIENCE AMERICA'S BEST WATER PARK

Water World is one of America's largest water parks. It is located about 20 minutes north of Denver. The park has 50 attractions, the largest variety of water attractions in America. There is something here for everyone in the family from thrilling water rides to children's play areas to wave pools. Water World is typically open from Memorial Day until Labor Day, but check online for opening times before you plan your visit. The park offers food and beverages in

\>TOURIST

the park, but I'd recommend packing a picnic and snacks to take in with you.

Water World has a variety of rides. You probably will not have enough time to ride them all, but I'd recommend making sure you at least go on Voyage to the Center of the Earth and Lost River of the Pharaohs. Voyage to the Center of the Earth is a dinosaur tube ride. You travel on a giant tube down a river, encountering dinosaurs along the way. This ride, along with the newer rides tend to have longer lines. River of the Pharaohs is similar to the dinosaur ride, but it is egyptian themed. It tends to have shorter lines than Voyage to the Center of the Earth, so be sure to check this one out as well.

If you are going as a family (2 adults and 2 kids), go to King Soopers, a grocery store close by, to pick up discount tickets. They will save you a couple of bucks and usually include free pizza and drinks. If your group is smaller, you can stop by Subway, and pick up coupons to save some money.

13. VISIT COLORADO'S MOST EXCITING RESTAURANT

You are not a true Coloradoan unless you've been to Casa Bonita. Casa Bonita is a Mexican Restaurant with a 30-foot waterfall. But it doesn't stop there. There are cliff divers, fire jugglers, mariachi bands, a pirate cave, magicians, puppet shows, a gorilla, and skeeball machines. And there is one thing that we all agree on: you don't go to Casa Bonita for the food. The food is decent but a little pricey for the quality you get. But, it's something you have to experience. As you take your seat and enjoy some Mexican food, a variety of short acts will perform. After dinner you can wander through the restaurant, exploring all of its treasures from the faces in the cliff to the pirate cave.

14. EXPERIENCE NATIVE AMERICAN FOOD

Tocabe is a Native American restaurant with the build your own benefits of Chipotle or Subway. You start by choosing your entree; I'd recommend getting an Indian Taco (think tostada but instead of a tortilla base, you get fry bread as your base). From there you'll walk through the line choosing your meat, beans, veggies, cheese, and salsa. Tocabe has amazing fry bread and divine meat. Staying true to Native American food, they serve Bison. Even though it is more expensive than the other meats, you have to try the shredded bison.

15. WEIGH IN ON THE GREEN CHILI DEBATE

Green chili is one of Denver's signature foods. Who serves the best green chili is a never-ending debate. Everyone has their own opinion on who serves the best green chili, but there are a few that stand out from the crowd: D'Corazon on Blake Street, Sam's No. 3 on Curtis Street, Breck on Blake Street, and Cherry Cricket in Cherry Creek. Try a few different ones and cast your vote on who you think has the best green chili.

16. EAT A VOODOO DOLL DOUGHNUT

That's right: a doughnut shaped like a Voodoo doll. VooDoo doughnuts, in Downtown Denver right off of Colfax, sells raspberry filled doughnuts shaped like voodoo dolls. The store is open 24 hours selling fresh baked doughnuts. They sell almost every doughnut imaginable from Oreo to bubble gum.

VooDoo is a cash-only establishment, so remember to have cash on hand. If you forget to bring cash, no worries, there is an ATM inside. Once you've been to Voodoo, you might notice other people in the airport carrying the pink doughnut boxes to bring doughnuts back to friends or family.

> *"And then there is the most dangerous risk of all — the risk of spending your life not doing what you want on the bet you can buy yourself the freedom to do it later."*
>
> – Randy Komisar

>TOURIST

17. GET A DRINK AT A CRAFT BREWERY

Almost everyone here brews their own beers. There are around 150 breweries in Denver and 350 in the state. With so many to choose from, there is something for every taste. One of my favorites is Great Divide Brewing Co. You can order a flight where you can try samples of the drinks they currently have on tap. You can also tour the brewery. It's a short tour, but interesting to see things on a smaller scale. If you are there in November, be sure to check out their Yeti Awareness Week. During Yeti Awareness Week, there are a variety of events happening from raffles to variations of their famous Yeti brew.

18. HIT SNOOZE

No, not the snooze on your alarm, Snooze the breakfast place. It is one of the most popular breakfast restaurants among locals serving up traditional breakfast foods along with some unique twists to our favorites. Unlike larger chains, they are very accommodating to special requests. Don't feel bad for making substitutions or deciding you want one breakfast taco, one pancake, and one french toast, they don't mind. Because it is a favorite, the wait can get really long. For the shortest wait, come before 9am or after 1pm. But no matter when you go, expect some kind of wait.

If pancakes are your thing, I'd suggest getting the pancake flight (a sample of three of their pancakes). If you get the pancake flight, I'd recommend getting the cinnamon roll pancake, pineapple upside down pancake, and whatever their special pancake is (my favorite has been lemon meringue). The cinnamon roll pancake is not always on the menu, but they should be able to make it for you, just ask!

If you are not into pancakes, try Juan's Breakfast Tacos. Juan's Breakfast Tacos are tortillas filled with scrambled eggs, hash browns, cheese, green chile hollandaise, and pico. While you are dining their delicious breakfast, take a look at the walls to find the hidden toys. See if you can find them!

19. BEHIND THE FREEZER DOOR

Frozen Matter is a micro-creamery that serves ice cream, popsicles, and soda. Their unique, small-batch ice cream is reason alone to go to Frozen Matter. But, ice cream is not the only reason to visit. In the back of the store is what looks to be a normal freezer door, but it is really the entrance to a hidden bar: Retrograde Bar. Beyond the walk-in freezer door, you'll find a chilly, purple-lit, mid-century modern bar. With a menu that matches the uniqueness of the bar itself, you can not go wrong here.

20. LITTLE MAN ICE CREAM

Taking inspiration from the Coney Island hot dog shaped stands, Little Man Ice Cream serves their delicious ice cream out of a 28-foot tall cream can. The unique building only adds to the amazing service and delicious ice cream served here. Dedicated to making a difference, Little Man donates a scoop of rice or beans to a community in need for every scoop of ice cream sold.

There really isn't really a best on the menu here since all of their ice cream is homemade and delicious. They offer some unique flavors though. So, if you are wanting to try something different, try a flavor like Purple Cow, Salted Oreo, or French Toast. The line can be long, but the ice cream at the end makes it worth it.

21. PUT YOUR VOTE IN FOR THE BEST BURRITO

There are burrito shops found on pretty much every corner in Denver. Here are a few local favorites: Illegal Pete's, Renegade Burrito, and Santiago's. Illegal Pete's has multiple Denver locations, so no matter where you are, there is one close to you. Their burritos are distinct and flavorful. If you only have time to go try one burrito place, go to Illegal Pete's.

Renegade Burrito has one of the best breakfast burritos. They offer flavored tortillas which add a unique twist to their delicious burritos. If you are in North Denver, be sure to stop by one of their locations.

>TOURIST

Santiago's is a staple in Colorado. Their burritos are delicious and inexpensive. If you are looking for a cheap and quick option, Santiago's is a great choice.

22. BURRITO PIZZA?

There are so many pizza options, it is hard to choose a favorite. With so many different styles and toppings, you really can't go wrong, but I just can't stop going back to Ian's and DP Dough.

Ian's offers traditional pizza as well as some more exciting combinations. My favorite is their mac n' cheese pizza (this also happens to be their best seller). They also have quesadilla, macadilla killa (a spiced up mac n' cheese), burrito, and loaded baked potato pizzas. They might sound weird at first, but they are genius! Located near Coors field, it is the perfect location to get a bite to eat before a Rockies game.

DP Dough does not sell traditional pizza, but calzones. Their unique store displays local artwork on the ceiling panels. DP Dough has a wide range of "zones" you can choose from, or you can create your own calzone. Be sure to order some cookies with your calzone as they bake the cookies fresh with your order.

23. ROCKY MOUNTAIN OYSTERS

Rocky Mountain Oysters are not oysters at all, they are typically breaded and fried bull or bison testicles. They usually have a gamey taste to them, similar to venison. Rocky Mountain Oysters were invented by ranchers in the Rocky Mountains as a cheap source of food since they were normally just thrown away. Young bulls are commonly castrated to regulate breeding, muscle growth, and temperament.

Many restaurants serve them, typically as an appetizer, but I'd recommend going to The Buckhorn Exchange, near Lincoln Park. The Buckhorn Exchange is a classic steakhouse celebrating frontier legends. They have been serving up meat since 1893, so they know what they are doing. Because they are one of the best, they come with a high price tag. If you are looking for a less expensive option to try the famous Rocky Mountain Oysters, you can find them at a number of local restaurants, including Coors Field.

24. FOOL'S GOLD

Most people associate the peanut butter, jelly (or banana), and bacon sandwich with Elvis Presley, but few know that it originated in Denver. Elvis tried the Fool's Gold Loaf and loved it. It was originally made with a full jar of jam, a full jar of peanut butter, and a pound of bacon inside a hollowed out loaf of bread. He loved it so much that when he was craving it, instead of making one in Tennessee, he jumped on his jet and flew to Denver to get another one of these massive sandwiches. The chef who made Elvis his first Fool's Gold Loaf still serves up smaller sized sandwiches of this novelty item at his restaurant, Nick's Cafe in Golden, just west of Denver.

25. VISIT THE ORIGINAL CHIPOTLE LOCATION

If you are a fan on Chipotle, you are in luck. The original Chipotle location is located in Denver near University of Denver's campus among other locally-owned food and coffee shops. It's a small location with an even smaller parking lot, so be prepared to park down the street and take your food to go. It may be the nostalgia, but something about the burritos here makes them taste a little bit better.

26. SHARK YOGA

The Downtown Aquarium, in Denver, houses more than 500 species of animals in exciting and engaging exhibits. In addition to the exhibits, the Downtown Aquarium has a full-service restaurant. Aside from traditional tanks, the aquarium has a train that takes visitors around the property, a carousel, and a 4D theater. They also have something unique to their aquarium: mermaids. Throughout the day, you can see the mermaids perform. Their shows are currently geared towards children, teaching them about the importance of conservation.

>TOURIST

Make sure to check their events calendar before you go incase they are hosting any of their unique events, like shark yoga or swimming with the sharks. To swim with the sharks you have to be scuba certified. If you're not certified, you can get your certification with just a few classes. When wandering through the aquarium, be sure to check out the sunken temple exhibit where you can learn how sunken ships and temple ruins provide homes for sea animals today.

27. DANCING AND BULL RIDING

One of the top country clubs, the Grizzly Rose, has a variety of live music and a great atmosphere. Every Wednesday night, The Grizzly Rose offers free line dance lessons: no cover charge, no reservations, just show up. If you can't make it there on a Wednesday, they have other dance classes throughout the week.

While you are there, you can test your strength on their mechanical bull. I have never been able to stay on very long, but it sure is fun to try. Generally, the weeknights are less crowded, unless a big name is playing a concert. Go to their website to check their concert line-up before you go. If you are traveling with anyone under 21, be sure to check the age requirements since they vary by day.

28. THE MUSIC SCENE

While Denver is no Nashville or New Orleans, it has an excellent music scene. The Americana and Indie scene are both growing rapidly here. In the past, Denver has been home to much larger, mainstream groups like One Republic, The Lumineers, and The Flobots.

You can check out the music scene by stopping at one of Denver's many music venues. The Hi-Dive and Larimer Lounge are both great places to go to experience live music.

29. DISCOVER THE HIDDEN ELVES

The Denver Museum of Nature and Science is a stellar museum. It has a wide variety of engaging exhibits to interest people of all ages. One of my all-time favorite exhibits is Expedition Health which

> TOURIST

teaches you about the human body. You learn about the importance of health, nutrition, and exercise through a variety of interactive stations. Another favorite is the wildlife exhibits which are detailed and fascinating. The exhibits are separated by region so you can see how the animals in each region interact with each other.

Many of the dioramas in the museum were painted by Kent Pendleton. Kent loved to hide tiny camouflaged gnomes or elves in his paintings. Try to see if you can spot any of the elves as you're looking at the paintings. After finding out about the hidden elves, the staff at the museum have added a few of their own elves. No one really knows how many elves are hidden in the museum, but try to find as many as you can. I've been able to find 8 so far. With so many exhibits and things to do, plan on spending most of your day here.

"A ship in a harbor is safe, but it not what ships are built for."

-John A. Shedd

30. RIDE A ROLLERCOASTER

There are two main amusement parks in Denver: Elitch Gardens and Lakeside Amusement Park. Elitch Gardens is the amusement park I grew up going to. It has a variety of thrilling rides, kid friendly rides, shows, and a water park. Elitch's is a great place to go if you only have one day to spend at a park since you can spend part of the day at the water park and the other at the theme park.

Elitch's also offers a rapid ride pass that allows you to get to the front of the line on most rides. While it is fairly expensive to add on, you will get your money's worth with the saved time. The rapid ride pass also includes one ride on either the XLR8R (150 ft free fall/swing) or the Slingshot. Both of these normally cost extra. Since you only get one, I'd recommend doing the XLR8R, it's a lot of fun and you can ride with two other people. Be sure to check out one of the shows at Elitch's or go to a dive-in movie. Their shows offer a variety of acts from magic to sword swallowing.

Lakeside is the older, vintage amusement park of Denver. It is cheaper than Elitch Gardens, but aside

>TOURIST

from the price, there are not many reasons to visit Lakeside over Elitch's. If you are looking for something more adventurous and a little farther out, try Glenwood Caverns Adventure Park. At Glenwood Caverns, among other things, you can swing off the side of a cliff.

31. SHOP LOCAL

During the summer months, Denver has multiple farmers markets. Two of my favorites are Cherry Creek Farmers Market and Union Station Farmers Market. Cherry Creek is Denver's largest and most awarded farmers market. It is usually open on Wednesdays and Saturdays, but try to go to the Saturday market as it has more vendors.

Union Station Farmers Market is in a very convenient location right outside of Union Station. It is typically open on Saturdays as well. A variety of local vendors and growers can be found at both markets. One of my favorite things to do is try local honey. Highland Honey (one of my favorites) frequents these farmer markets. The honey is made and packaged in Boulder, Colorado. They consistently have delicious honey. With so many different options, try going around lunchtime to have a meal of snacks and samples. Farmers markets are a great way to experience the local cuisine and support the local community.

32. WATCH HOW HOMEMADE CANDY IS MADE

Give in to your sweet side and learn how candy is made. Hammond's Candy Factory ships candy canes and other sweets all around the world. No matter where you are, if you see a Hammond's candy, it is made in the Denver factory.

To share their hand pulled craft, they give free tours every thirty minutes. At the start of the tour, you'll watch a video about the history of Hammond's. After that, they will bring you into a viewing area where you can watch candies being made. Hammond's is one of the only factories that still hand pulls their candies. You can see the process from mixing to pulling to packaging.

> TOURIST

Try to go during the week as the factory is typically busier and you'll get to see more candies being made. At the end of the tour, everyone will receive a free sample. The samples are candies that they can no longer sell because they are broken. Even though the samples are broken, they are still delicious. The tour conveniently ends in the gift shop. The gift shop has all of the sweets they make in the store as well as shirts and other gifts. Make sure to try a Mitchell's Sweet which is a homemade marshmallow covered in caramel. You may want to grab a few extra, they are addicting.

If you visit in December, Hammond's holds an annual candy cane festival. You can score some deals on their candy canes as well as visit Santa Claus. No matter when you visit Hammond's be sure to check out their deals, you can sometimes score candy canes for more than half off. Hard candy lasts a long time and makes for a great souvenir to bring home.

33. TAKE TIME FOR A PICNIC

City Park is one of the most popular parks in Denver, and for a good reason. It is also one of my favorites because it's where I got engaged. It is 320 acres and has a variety of recreational activities nearby. City Park is situated right by the Colorado Museum of Nature and Science and the Denver Zoo. Both are great if you have time.

The best time to visit City Park is during the summer. During the summer months, the park is busy with recreational sports, free concerts, and paddle boats (some of which are shaped like swans). City Park is just one of the many parks in Denver. If you have time, pack a picnic and enjoy the outdoors.

34. BIG BLUE BEAR

One of the most iconic art installations in Denver is "I See What You Mean" or more commonly known as the Big Blue Bear. The 40-foot, blue bear peeking inside of the convention center is hard to miss. The piece was created by Lawrence Argent who was commissioned to make a sculpture that represented Denver while avoiding cliches. He felt that the

>TOURIST

curious bear would catch the attention of onlookers, making them wonder what was going on inside of the Denver Convention Center.

The inspiration came to him when he was looking at a picture in the news of a bear peeking into a Colorado resident's home. The bear was originally supposed to be colored something more natural, like sandstone, but when a design print was accidentally printed in blue, Argent loved it. He immediately changed the bear's color to blue. Make sure to visit the Big Blue Bear to get a picture and post it using #bigbluebear.

35. OBSERVE THE ART SCENE

Take a few hours to enjoy some of the art Denver has to offer. You can visit one of the many museums or drive around to see street art. The Clyfford Still Museum displays a variety of Still's paintings from early on in his career to later in his life. You can view his development as a painter as you follow his paintings in chronological order. Though this is a lesser known museum, it is well worth the couple hours it takes to view. Some of the other popular art museums in Denver are the Denver Art Museum and the Denver Contemporary Art Museum.

If you opt to drive around to see local street art, some of the best places are RiNo (River North Art District), Confluence Park, and East Colfax. If you want to have a local show you around, look into doing a 2-hour tour from Denver Graffiti Tour. Denver Graffiti Tour knows their way around town. They will take you to popular and lesser known street art locations.

36. DISCOVER HOW TEA IS MADE

About an hour away from Denver is Boulder. Boulder is known for so many things, but one of my favorite things to do there is to visit Celestial Seasonings. Celestial Seasonings is one of the largest manufacturers of herbal teas in the world. They offer a free tour for you to learn how their world-famous tea is made. Tours run all day long.

When you first get to Celestial Seasonings, you'll check in at the front desk where you'll receive your

>TOURIST

ticket for the tour (a three pack tea sample) and a teacup. As you wait for your tour to begin, you can use your teacup to sample every tea Celestial Seasonings makes. Their tea counter has around ten different ready to drink teas. If you are wanting a different flavor, just order a free sample from the counter and they'll give you a fresh tea bag and hot water. If you run out of time to try teas before your tour starts, come back to the tour desk after your tour and ask for a new teacup. Be sure to try the SleepyTime Tea as this is one of their most popular teas. Some of my other favorites are Black Cherry, Raspberry Zinger, and Mint.

When your tour gets called, you'll be led into the video room where you'll learn more about the company's history and receive your hair net to go into the factory. Don't worry about looking funny in your hair net, everyone has to wear one. The tour guide will lead your group around the factory where you will watch the process of tea bags being made. They take you through every step: cleaning, mixing, bagging, packaging, and shipping.

One of the highlights of the tour is the Peppermint Room. All mint herbs have to be kept in a separate room so they do not make everything else smell like peppermint. The oils in mint are so strong that it makes your eyes water (unless you're wearing contacts). This tour once again conveniently ends in the gift shop where you can buy clothing, tea, and other gifts.

37. CATCH A TOP-NOTCH PERFORMANCE

The Denver Performing Arts Center is the second largest performing arts center in the nation. It showcases top-notch performances like Broadway plays, ballets, concerts, and more. I've seen a variety of performances here, but the Broadway performances always top the list. I've seen Mama Mia and Wicked and they were both fantastic. The shows frequently change. You check online to see your options.

If you see a show, there are a lot of great dining options close by. Many restaurants offer deals if you show them your show ticket. The deals range from a free dessert to half off drinks to discounted appetizers

>TOURIST

and more. Be sure to check online to view all of your options.

38. CHALK ART FESTIVAL

Out of all of the Denver festivals, the Denver Chalk Art Festival is one of my favorites. More than 200 artists create beautiful pieces of art out of chalk right on the pavement. The artists spend hours on end leaning over and standing on boards as to not smudge their works of art. The tradition of chalk art traces back to Italy, so you will also find Italian food and music at the festival. If you are in Denver for both days of the festival, try to go back multiple times so you can see how the artists' works have progressed.

39. DENVER BOTANIC GARDENS

Rated one of the top 5 gardens to visit in the nation, the Denver Botanic Gardens is an amazing place to visit. Throughout the year, the gardens features seasonal items and local artist exhibits. The gardens are absolutely beautiful and are continually changing. Even if you have visited the garden before, chances are you will have a different experience than the first time you came.

The gardens have plenty of benches, so if you get tired, you can take a break and enjoy the scenery. Try to time your visit around lunchtime and have lunch at Hive Bistro. The food at Hive Bistro is delicious, and when possible, they source ingredients from the garden.

There are two different locations, York Street (zoned gardens and greenhouse) and Chatfield (garden and flowers). Both are stunning gardens, but if you can only go to one, I'd suggest the York Street location since it is the main location.

"Not all those who wander are lost."

– J.R.R. Tolkien

>TOURIST

40. THE UNSINKABLE MOLLY BROWN

Denver was home to "The Unsinkable Molly Brown", a Titanic survivor. Her house is now a museum of her life as well as preserving Victorian-era architecture. Molly Brown came to Denver with her brother during the gold rush. It was here that she became an activist and met her husband. They became millionaires almost overnight when her husband struck gold. With some of this fortune, they purchased the home that is now known as the Molly Brown House and Museum. Tours are about 45 minutes and go through the life and impact of Molly Brown. You'll learn that surviving the Titanic was only one of the many great accomplishments of Molly Brown.

41. SPORTS

As an active city, we love sports which shows as we have 7 professional sports teams. With 7 professional sports teams, there is always a game to watch. We have the Denver Broncos (NFL), Denver Nuggets (NBA), Colorado Avalanche (NHL), Colorado Rockies (MLB), Colorado Rapids (MLS),

Colorado Outlaws (MLL), and Colorado Mammoth (NLL). No matter when you go, there will be a game for you to enjoy. If you don't want to spend a lot on tickets, most of the games have inexpensive rickets so you can go and enjoy the atmosphere.

Aside from going to a sports game, you can take a tour through the Broncos' stadium or go through the National Ballpark Museum. The Denver Broncos' stadium has tours during the day. The tour takes about an hour and a half and lets you tour parts of the stadium that aren't normally open to the public including the locker rooms and press room.

The National Ballpark Museum is right across from Coors Field. The museum takes you through baseball history. Bruce Hellerstein started collecting baseball cards but soon obtained larger items like old stadium chairs and uniforms. He displayed his collection in his basement until 2010 when it moved to its current location. With so many great things to see, it is a great way to spend an hour of your time in Denver.

>TOURIST

42. NATIONAL WESTERN STOCK SHOW

Held every year in January, for 16 days, the National Western Stock Show is something you have to experience. It is one of the world's largest and most diverse rodeos, attracting over 650,000 visitors. The Stock Show hosts a variety of events and competitions beyond the typical riding broncos and roping calves. One of my favorite events is Xtreme Dogs. They do a variety of agility, herding, and retrieving competitions with dogs of all different breeds. Even if you are not into the traditional rodeo events, the National Western Stock Show has a lot to offer.

43. COLORADO CANNABIS

While many other states have since legalized weed, Colorado will probably always be known for it. If you are wanting to participate, you can find dispensaries all around Denver selling everything from pre-rolled joints to gourmet edibles. If you don't know what you are doing, ask questions, the workers will be more than happy to answer your questions.

If you're wanting to experience the weed culture but don't want to participate there are a few options out there. Cheba Hut is a weed-themed sandwich shop. The names of their menu items have some kind of marijuana reference. Denver is also home to the International Church of Cannabis, a colorful, repurposed building. Members are known as Elevationists who, through ritual and guidance, use cannabis to reveal their best selves. You can tour their property Friday - Sunday, but because of local laws, you can not consume weed during the times it is open to the public.

No matter what you do, keep in mind that there are still laws in place as far as who can have it, the amounts you can have, and where you can have it. Just because marijuana is legal does not mean it is legal everywhere for everyone.

>TOURIST

44. GREAT AMERICAN BEER FESTIVAL

The Great American Beer Festival is the beer festival. It is a tasting event as well as a competition. Serving the largest number of beers, you can (theoretically) try over 4,000 samples. Samples are served in one-ounce cups enabling you to taste a variety of brews. If you are going in a group, one of you can buy a "designated driver ticket" which is available for less than half the price and gives the holder a variety of non-alcoholic drink options. If you are visiting in October, put The Great American Beer Festival on your list of things to do.

45. COORS BREWERY

Coors Brewery in Golden is about 25 minutes away from Denver. It is the largest single-site brewery in the world. On their free 30 minute tour, you'll learn everything from brewing to packaging. They have been brewing beer for over 100 years, since 1873. The tour focuses on their history and passion that has led Coors to be what we know it as today.

As part of the tour, you get to sample their beer. For everyone under 21, they provide a non-alcoholic option, typically lemonade. At the end of the tour there is a little museum of old bottles and memorabilia that is fun to look at. Even if you do not drink beer, the tour is very fascinating, and it's free!

46. THE MILE HIGH CITY

Denver really is the Mile High City. The 13th step on the west side of the capitol building is exactly 1 mile above sea level. Make sure to visit the capitol building and get your #milehigh picture. In addition to being a mile high, the capitol building is filled with a unique history. The building itself is made from Colorado Rose Onyx, a stone that is incredibly rare. All of the known Colorado Rose Onyx was used in the construction of the capitol building.

You can learn more about the Denver Capitol Building by taking a free tour. The tours are usually offered during the day, Monday - Friday. For up-to-date tour information, visit their website online. In pre-school my class got a private tour of the capitol building which included going to the very top. We got

>TOURIST

to go because one of my classmate's father was the mayor. I didn't know at the time that anyone could tour the building, so I felt pretty special getting to go inside a "secret government building."

47. STROLL DOWN HISTORICAL LARIMER SQUARE

Larimer Square is Denver's oldest and most historic block. It has a variety of independent shops, unique restaurants, and lively nightlife. Be sure to visit at night to see the block at its peak with a canopy of lights.

The block is filled with history. In 1861, when Colorado became a territory, Larimer Street was Denver City's main street. Every shop has its own unique history. Some of the buildings were the sites of the first log cabins in Colorado while another is the site of the first Post Office in Denver. Go online to view each building's unique history. You can also find special events happening at Larimer Square on their website.

48. SHOP 16TH STREET MALL

16th Street Mall is Denver's mile long, outdoor mall. It is filled with restaurants, stores, and attractions. A free shuttle bus runs up and down the mall in case you get tired of walking. If you are looking for a more exciting way to travel, you can rent a horse-drawn carriage or pedicab.

Make sure to try a burger at the 5280 Burger Bar. In case you didn't pick up on the reference, 5280 is referring to the mile high city since there are 5,280 feet in a mile. 5280 Burger Bar uses Colorado beef and has 12 Colorado craft beers on tap.

16th Street Mall has something for everyone. The food ranges from street food to a nice sit-down restaurant. The shops are unique and offer one of a kind souvenirs. If you are looking for a local souvenir shop, stop by I Heart Denver. The store supports more than 150 artists so you are not only getting a unique gift, but also supporting the local community.

If you are looking for something to satisfy your sweet tooth, there are many great options. One to look out for is Santa Fe Cookies. Santa Fe Cookies bakes up delicious small batch cookies. Their store is only cash and relies on the honor system. To pay, you just drop your money in a bucket and grab your cookies so make sure you have a few extra dollars on you!

49. FIND OUT HOW MONEY IS MADE

We rarely think of how our money is made, we just use it. Until recently, I did not realize that there are only four US mints. Denver just happens to have one of them. The Denver Mint is also the largest coin producer in the world. The United States Mint offers free, 45-minute guided tours where you can learn the process and history behind money making in America.

While tour tickets are free, they are limited so you have to plan accordingly. The Mint offers six tours a day. Tickets are distributed on a first come first served basis. There is no way to make reservations here. The ticket window opens in the morning, so be sure to wake up early to ensure you get a tour time. Visit the US Mint's website for the most up-to-date information on ticket window opening times and closures.

The tour has a number of restrictions to keep in mind. The tour is only available to adults and children over the age of 7. Security is a top priority so you will not be allowed to bring anything larger than a cell phone in with you, so be sure to leave any backpacks or purses in the car or hotel. To see a full list of rules, check online.

If you want to learn more about money, you can also visit the Federal Reserve Museum. Here you will learn about the nation's financial system and its impact. As a unique souvenir, you can get a bag of shredded money.

50. GET A GLIMPSE OF BLUCIFER

The Denver Airport is full of conspiracy theories and stories, but Blucifer is probably the most well known. Officially named Blue Mustang, the horse has been given then name Blucifer (Blue+Lucifer) because of the common belief that the statue is cursed or demonic.

Luis Jimenez designed Blue Mustang to represent the state's Old American West spirit. When a section of the 9,000-pound horse fell on Luis's leg, severing an artery, it killed him. Despite Jimenez's death, the statue was finished and finally displayed at Denver International Airport.

The horse's glowing red eyes only add to the belief that the statue is cursed. Some also believe that Blucifer is meant to represent the fourth horseman of the apocalypse which represents death. Blucifer is just one of the many conspiracy theories surrounding the Denver International Airport. If this is something that interests you, there are many articles and youtube videos going into more detail.

> *"The world is a book and those who do not travel read only one page."*
>
> – Augustine of Hippo

>TOURIST

TOP REASONS TO BOOK THIS TRIP

Mountains: The Rocky Mountains are the backyard of Denver.

Sports: With 7 professional leagues and a a variety of outdoor sports, Denver is a sports meca.

Food: Denver has a variety of amazing food.

History: A rich history makes Denver a must-see location for history buffs.

OTHER RESOURCES:

https://www.denver.org/

>TOURIST

BONUS BOOK

50 THINGS TO KNOW ABOUT PACKING LIGHT FOR TRAVEL

PACK THE RIGHT WAY EVERY TIME

AUTHOR: MANIDIPA BHATTACHARYYA

First Published in 2015 by Dr. Lisa Rusczyk. Copyright 2015. All Rights Reserved. No part of this publication may be reproduced, including scanning and photocopying, or distributed in any form or by any means, electronic or mechanical, or stored in a database or retrieval system without prior written permission from the publisher.

Disclaimer: The publisher has put forth an effort in preparing and arranging this book. The information provided herein by the author is provided "as is". Use this information at your own risk. The publisher is not a licensed doctor. Consult your doctor before engaging in any medical activities. The publisher and author disclaim any liabilities for any loss of profit or commercial or personal damages resulting from the information contained in this book.

Edited by Melanie Howthorne

ABOUT THE AUTHOR

Manidipa Bhattacharyya is a creative writer and editor, with an education in English literature and Linguistics. After working in the IT industry for seven long years she decided to call it quits and follow her heart instead. Manidipa has been ghost writing, editing, proof reading and doing secondary research services for many story tellers and article writers for about three years. She stays in Kolkata, India with her husband and a busy two year old. In her own time Manidipa enjoys travelling, photography and writing flash fiction.

Manidipa believes in travelling light and never carries anything that she couldn't haul herself on a trip. However, travelling with her child changed the scenario. She seemed to carry the entire world with her for the baby on the first two trips. But good sense prevailed and she is again working her way to becoming a light traveler, this time with a kid.

INTRODUCTION

*He who would travel happily
must travel light.*

-Antoine de Saint-Exupéry

Travel takes you to different places from seas and mountains to deserts and much more. In your travels you get to interact with different people and their cultures. You will, however, enjoy the sights and interact positively with these new people even more, if you are travelling light.

When you travel light your mind can be free from worry about your belongings. You do not have to spend precious vacation time waiting for your luggage to arrive after a long flight. There is be no chance of your bags going missing and the best part is that you need not pay a fee for checked baggage.

People who have mastered this art of packing light will root for you to take only one carry-on, wherever you go. However, many people can find it really hard to pack light. More so if you are travelling with children. Differentiating between "must have" and "just in case" items is the starting point. There will be ample shopping avenues at your destination which are just waiting to be explored.

This book will show you 'packing' in a new 'light' – pun intended – and help you to embrace light packing practices for all of your future travels.

Off to packing!

DEDICATION

I dedicate this book to all the travel buffs that I know, who have given me great insights into the contents of their backpacks.

THE RIGHT TRAVEL GEAR

1. CHOOSE YOUR TRAVEL GEAR CAREFULLY

While selecting your travel gear, pick items that are light weight, durable and most importantly, easy to carry. There are cases with wheels so you can drag them along – these are usually on the heavy side because of the trolley. Alternatively a backpack that you can carry comfortably on your back, or even a duffel bag that you can carry easily by hand or sling across your body are also great options. Whatever you choose, one thing to keep in mind is that the luggage itself should not weigh a ton, this will give you the flexibility to bring along one extra pair of shoes if you so desire.

2. CARRY THE MINIMUM NUMBER OF BAGS

Selecting light weight luggage is not everything. You need to restrict the number of bags you carry as well. One carry-on size bag is ideal for light travel. Most carriers allow one cabin baggage plus one purse, handbag or camera bag as long as it slides under the seat in front. So technically, you can carry two items of luggage without checking them in.

3. PACK ONE EXTRA BAG

Always pack one extra empty bag along with your essential items. This could be a very light weight duffel bag or even a sturdy tote bag which takes up minimal space. In the event that you end up buying a lot of souvenirs, you already have a handy bag to stuff all that into and do not have to spend time hunting for an appropriate bag.

> *I'm very strict with my packing and have everything in its right place. I never change a rule. I hardly use anything in the hotel room. I wheel my own wardrobe in and that's it.*
>
> Charlie Watts

CLOTHES & ACCESSORIES

4. PLAN AHEAD

Figure out in advance what you plan to do on your trip. That will help you to pick that one dress you need for the occasion. If you are going to attend a wedding then you have to carry formal wear. If not, you can ditch the gown for something lighter that will be comfortable during long walks or on the beach.

5. WEAR THAT JACKET

Remember that wearing items will not add extra luggage for your air travel. So wear that bulky jacket that you plan to carry for your trip. This saves space and can also help keep you warm during the chilly flight.

6. MIX AND MATCH

Carry clothes that can be interchangeably used to reinvent your look. Find one top that goes well with a couple of pairs of pants or skirts. Use tops, shirts and jackets wisely along with other accessories like a scarf or a stole to create a new look.

7. CHOOSE YOUR FABRIC WISELY

Stuffing clothes in cramped bags definitely takes its toll which results in wrinkles. It is best to carry wrinkle free, synthetic clothes or merino tops. This will eliminate the need for that small iron you usually bring along.

8. DITCH CLOTHES PACK UNDERWEAR

Pack more underwear and socks. These are the things that will give you a fresh feel even if you do not get a chance to wear fresh clothes. Moreover these are easy to wash and can be dried inside the hotel room itself.

9. CHOOSE DARK OVER LIGHT

While picking your clothes choose dark coloured ones. They are easy to colour coordinate and can last longer before needing a wash. Accidental food spills and dirt from the road are less visible on darker clothes.

10. WEAR YOUR JEANS

Take only one pair of Jeans with you, which you should wear on the flight. Remember to pick a pair that can be worn for sightseeing trips and is equally eloquent for dinner. You can add variety by adding light weight cargoes and chinos.

11. CARRY SMART ACCESSORIES

The right accessory can give you a fresh look even with the same old dress. An intelligent neck-piece, a couple of bright scarves, stoles or a sarong can be used in a number of ways to add variety to your clothing. These light weight beauties can double up as a nursing cover, a light blanket, beach wear, a modesty cover for visiting places of worship, and also makes for an enthralling game of peek-a-boo.

12. LEARN TO FOLD YOUR GARMENTS

Seasoned travellers all swear by rolling their clothes for compact and wrinkle free packing. Bundle packing, where you roll the clothes around a central object as if tying it up, is also a popular method of compact and wrinkle free packing. Stacking folded clothes one on top of another is a big no-no as it makes creases extreme and they are difficult to get rid of without ironing.

>TOURIST

13. WASH YOUR DIRTY LAUNDRY

One of the ways to avoid carrying loads of clothes is to wash the clothes you carry. At some places you might get to use the laundry services or a Laundromat but if you are in a pinch, best solution is to wash them yourself. If that is the plan then carrying quick drying clothes is highly recommended, which most often also happen to be the wrinkle free variety.

14. LEAVE THOSE TOWELS BEHIND

Regular towels take up a lot of space, are heavy and take ages to dry out. If you are staying at hotels they will provide you with towels anyway. If you are travelling to a remote place, where the availability of towels look doubtful, carry a light weight travel towel of viscose material to do the job.

15. USE A COMPRESSION BAG

Compression bags are getting lots of recommendation now days from regular travellers. These are useful for saving space in your luggage when you have to pack bulky dresses. While packing for the return trip, get help from the hotel staff to arrange a vacuum cleaner.

FOOTWEAR

16. PUT ON YOUR HIKING BOOTS

If you have plans to go hiking or trekking during your trip, you will need those bulky hiking boots. The best way to carry them is to wear them on flight to save space and luggage weight. You can remove the boots once inside and be comfortable in your socks.

17. PICKING THE RIGHT SHOES

Shoes are often the bulkiest items, along with being the dainty if you are a female. They need care and take up a lot of space in your luggage. It is advisable therefore to pick shoes very carefully. If you plan to do a lot of walking and site seeing, then wearing a pair of comfortable walking shoes are a must. For more formal occasions you can carry durable, light weight flats which will not take up much space.

18. STUFF SHOES

If you happen to pack a pair of shoes, ensure you utilize their hollow insides. Tuck small items like rolled up socks or belts to save space. They will also be easy to find.

>TOURIST

TOILETRIES

19. STASHING TOILETRIES

Carry only absolute necessities. Airline rules dictate that for one carry-on bag, liquids and gels must be in 3.4 ounce (100ml) bottles or less, and must be packed in a one quart zip-lock bag. If you are planning to stay in a hotel, the basic things will be provided for you. It's best is to buy the rest from the local market at your destination.

20. TAKE ALONG TAMPONS

Tampons are a hard to find item in a lot of countries. Figure out how many you need and pack accordingly. For longer stays you can buy them online and have them delivered to where you are staying.

21. GET PAMPERED BEFORE YOU TRAVEL

Some avid travellers suggest getting a pedicure and manicure just the day before travelling. This not only gives you a well kept look, you also save the trouble of packing nail polish. Remember, every little bit of weight reduced adds up.

ELECTRONICS

22. LUGGING ALONG ELECTRONICS

Electronics have a large role to play in our lives today. Most of us cannot imagine our lives away from our phones, laptops or tablets. However while travelling, one must consider the amount of weight these electronics add to our luggage. Thankfully smart phones come along with all the essentials tools like a camera, email access, picture editing tools and more. They are smart to the point of eliminating the need to carry multiple gadgets. Choose a smart phone that suits all your requirements and travel with the world in your palms or pocket.

23. REDUCE THE NUMBER OF CHARGERS

If you do travel with multiple electronic devices, you will have to bear the additional burden of carrying all their chargers too. Check if a single charger can be used for multiple devices. You might also consider investing in a pocket charger. These small devices support multiple devices while keeping you charged on the go.

> TOURIST

24. TRAVEL FRIENDLY APPS

Along with smart phones come numerous apps, which are immensely helpful in our travels. You name it and you have an app for it at hand – take pictures, sharing with friends and family, torch to light dark roads, maps, checking flight/train times, find hotels and many other things. Use these smart alternatives to traditional items like books to eliminate weight and save space.

I get ideas about what's essential when packing my suitcase.

-Diane von Furstenberg

TRAVELLING WITH KIDS

25. BRING ALONG THE STROLLER

Kids might enjoy walking for a while but they soon tire out and a stroller is the just the right thing for them to rest in while you continue your tour. Strollers also double duty as a luggage carrier and shopping bag holder. Remember to pick a light weight, easy to handle brand of stroller. Better yet, find out in advance if you can rent a stroller at your destination.

26. BRING ONLY ENOUGH DIAPERS FOR YOUR TRIP

Diapers take up a lot of space and add to the weight of your luggage. Therefore it is advisable to carry just enough diapers to last through the trip and a few for afterwards, till you buy fresh stock at your destination. Unless of course you are travelling to a really remote area, in which case you have no choice but to carry the load. Otherwise diapers are something you will find pretty easily.

27. TAKE ONLY A COUPLE OF TOYS

Children are easily attracted by new things in their environment. While travelling they will find numerous 'new' objects to scrutinize and play with. Packing just one favorite toy is enough, or if there is no favorite toy leave out all of them in favor of stories or imaginary games.

28. CARRY KID FRIENDLY SNACKS

Create a small snack counter in your bag to store away quick bites for those sudden hunger pangs. Depending on the child's age this could include chocolates, raisins, dry fruits, granola bars or biscuits. Also keep a bottle of water handy for your little one.

These things do not add much weight and can be adjusted in a handbag or knapsack.

29. GAMES TO CARRY

Create some travel specific, imaginary games if you have slightly grown up children, like spot the attractions. Keep a coloring book and colors handy for in-flight or hotel time. Apps on your smart phone can keep the children engaged with cartoons and story books. Older children are often entertained by games available on phones or tablets. This cuts the weight of luggage down while keeping the kids entertained.

30. LET THE KIDS CARRY THEIR LOAD

A good thing is to start early sharing of responsibilities. Let your child pick a bag of his or her choice and pack it themselves. Keep tabs on what they are stuffing in their bags by asking if they will be using that item on the trip. It could start out being just an entertainment bag initially but with growing years they will learn to sort the useful from the superfluous. Children as little as four can maneuver a small trolley suitcase like a pro- their experience in pull along toys credit. If you are worried that you may be pulling it for them, you may want to start with a backpack.

31. DECIDE ON LOCATION FOR CHILDREN TO SLEEP

While on a trip you might not always get a crib at your destination, and carrying one will make life all the more difficult. Instead call ahead to see if there are any cribs or roll out beds for children. You may even put blankets on the floor. Weave them a story about camping and they will gladly sleep without any trouble.

32. GET BABY PRODUCTS DELIVERED AT YOUR DESTINATION

If you are absolutely paranoid about not getting your favourite variety of diaper or brand of baby food, check out online stores like amazon.com for services in your destination city. You can buy things online ahead of your travel and get them delivered to your hotel upon arrival.

33. FEEDING NEEDS OF YOUR INFANTS

If you are travelling with a breastfed infant, you save the trouble of carrying bottles and bottle sanitization kits. For special food, or medications, you may need

>TOURIST

to call ahead to make sure you have a refrigerator where you are staying.

34. FEEDING NEEDS OF YOUR TODDLER

With the progression from infancy to toddler, their dietary requirements too evolve. You will have to pack some snacks for travelling time. Fresh fruits and vegetables can be purchased at your destination. Most of the cities you travel to in whichever part of the world, will have baby food products and formulas, available at the local drug-store or the supermarket.

35. PICKING CLOTHES FOR YOUR BABY

Contrary to popular belief, babies can do without many changes of clothes. At the most pack 2 outfits per day. Pack mix and match type clothes for your little one as well. Pick things which are comfortable to wear and quick to dry.

36. SELECTING SHOES FOR YOUR BABY

Like outfits, kids can make do with two pairs of comfortable shoes. If you can get some water resistant shoes it will be best. To expedite drying wet shoes, you can stuff newspaper in them then wrap them with newspaper and leave them to dry overnight.

37. KEEP ONE CHANGE OF CLOTHES HANDY

Travelling with kids can be tricky. Keep a change of clothes for the kids and mum handy in your purse or tote bag. This takes a bit of space in your hand luggage but comes extremely handy in case there are any accidents or spills.

38. LEAVE BEHIND BABY ACCESSORIES

Baby accessories like their bed, bath tub, car seat, crib etc. should be left at home. Many hotels provide a crib on request, while car seats can be borrowed from friends or rented. Babies can be given a bath in the hotel sink or even in the adult bath tub with a little bit of water. If you bring a few bath toys, they can be used in the bath, pool, and out of water. They can also be sanitized easily in the sink.

39. CARRY A SMALL LOAD OF PLASTIC BAGS

With children around there are chances of a number of soiled clothes and diapers. These plastic bags help to sort the dirt from the clean inside your big bag.

These are very light weight and come in handy to other carry stuff as well at times.

PACK WITH A PURPOSE

40. PACKING FOR BUSINESS TRIPS

One neutral-colored suit should suffice. It can be paired with different shirts, ties and accessories for different occasions. One pair of black suit pants could be worn with a matching jacket for the office or with a snazzy top for dinner.

41. PACKING FOR A CRUISE

Most cruises have formal dinners, and that formal dress usually takes up a lot of space. However you might find a tuxedo to rent. For women, a short black dress with multiple accessory options will do the trick.

42. PACKING FOR A LONG TRIP OVER DIFFERENT CLIMATES

The secret packing mantra for travel over multiple climates is layering. Layering traps air around your body creating insulation against the cold. The same light t-shirt that is comfortable in a warmer climate can be the innermost layer in a colder climate.

REDUCE SOME MORE WEIGHT

43. LEAVE PRECIOUS THINGS AT HOME

Things that you would hate to lose or get damaged leave them at home. Precious jewelry, expensive gadgets or dresses, could be anything. You will not require these on your trip. Leave them at home and spare the load on your mind.

44. SEND SOUVENIRS BY MAIL

If you have spent all your money on purchasing souvenirs, carrying them back in the same bag that you brought along would be difficult. Either pack everything in another bag and check it in the airport or get everything shipped to your home. Use an international carrier for a secure transit, but this could be more expensive than the checking fees at the airport.

45. AVOID CARRYING BOOKS

Books equal to weight. There are many reading apps which you can download on your smart phone or tab.

Plus there are gadgets like Kindle and Nook that are thinner and lighter alternatives to your regular book.

CHECK, GET, SET, CHECK AGAIN

46. STRATEGIZE BEFORE PACKING

Create a travel list and prepare all that you think you need to carry along. Keep everything on your bed or floor before packing and then think through once again – do I really need that? Any item that meets this question can be avoided. Remove whatever you don't really need and pack the rest.

47. TEST YOUR LUGGAGE

Once you have fully packed for the trip take a test trip with your luggage. Take your bags and go to town for window shopping for an hour. If you enjoy your hour long trip it is good to go, if not, go home and reduce the load some more. Repeat this test till you hit the right weight.

48. ADD A ROLL OF DUCT TAPE

You might wonder why, when this book has been talking about reducing stuff, we're suddenly asking you to pack something totally unusual. This is because when you have limited supplies, duct tape is immensely helpful for small repairs – a broken bag, leaking zip-lock bag, broken sunglasses, you name it and duct tape can fix it, temporarily.

49. LIST OF ESSENTIAL ITEMS

Even though the emphasis is on packing light, there are things which have to be carried for any trip. Here is our list of essentials:

- Passport/Visa or any other ID

- Any other paper work that might be required on a trip like permits, hotel reservation confirmations etc.

- Medicines – all your prescription medicines and emergency kit, especially if you are travelling with children

- Medical or vaccination records

- Money in foreign currency if travelling to a different country

- Tickets- Email or Message them to your phone

50. MAKE THE MOST OF YOUR TRIP

Wherever you are going, whatever you hope to do we encourage you to embrace it whole-heartedly. Take in the scenery, the culture and above all, enjoy your time away from home.

On a long journey even a straw weighs heavy.

-Spanish Proverb

>TOURIST

PACKING AND PLANNING TIPS

A Week before Leaving

- Arrange for someone to take care of pets and water plants.
- Stop mail and newspaper.
- Notify Credit Card companies where you are going.
- Change your thermostat settings.
- Car inspected, oil is changed, and tires have the correct pressure.
- Passports and photo identification is up to date.
- Pay bills.
- Copy important items and download travel Apps.
- Start collecting small bills for tips.

Right Before Leaving

- Clean out refrigerator.
- Empty garbage cans.
- Lock windows.
- Make sure you have the proper identification with you.
- Bring cash for tips.
- Remember travel documents.
- Lock door behind you.
- Remember wallet.
- Unplug items in house and pack chargers.

>TOURIST

READ OTHER GREATER THAN A TOURIST BOOKS

Greater Than a Tourist San Miguel de Allende Guanajuato Mexico: 50 Travel Tips from a Local by Tom Peterson

Greater Than a Tourist – Lake George Area New York USA: 50 Travel Tips from a Local by Janine Hirschklau

Greater Than a Tourist – Monterey California United States: 50 Travel Tips from a Local by Katie Begley

Greater Than a Tourist – Chanai Crete Greece: 50 Travel Tips from a Local by Dimitra Papagrigoraki

Greater Than a Tourist – The Garden Route Western Cape Province South Africa: 50 Travel Tips from a Local by Li-Anne McGregor van Aardt

Greater Than a Tourist – Sevilla Andalusia Spain: 50 Travel Tips from a Local by Gabi Gazon

Greater Than a Tourist – Kota Bharu Kelantan Malaysia: 50 Travel Tips from a Local by Aditi Shukla

Children's Book: Charlie the Cavalier Travels the World by Lisa Rusczyk

>TOURIST

> TOURIST

Visit Greater Than a Tourist for Free Travel Tips
http://GreaterThanATourist.com

Sign up for the Greater Than a Tourist Newsletter for discount days, new books, and travel information:
http://eepurl.com/cxspyf

Follow us on Facebook for tips, images, and ideas:
https://www.facebook.com/GreaterThanATourist

Follow us on Pinterest for travel tips and ideas:
http://pinterest.com/GreaterThanATourist

Follow us on Instagram for beautiful travel images:
http://Instagram.com/GreaterThanATourist

>TOURIST

> TOURIST

Please leave your honest review of this book on Amazon and Goodreads. Please send your feedback to GreaterThanaTourist@gmail.com as we continue to improve the series. We appreciate your positive and constructive feedback. Thank you.

>TOURIST

METRIC CONVERSIONS

TEMPERATURE

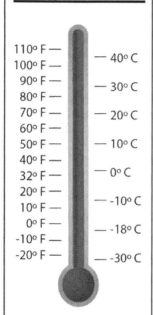

110° F — 40° C
100° F —
90° F — 30° C
80° F —
70° F — 20° C
60° F —
50° F — 10° C
40° F —
32° F — 0° C
20° F —
10° F — -10° C
0° F —
-10° F — -18° C
-20° F — -30° C

To convert F to C:

Subtract 32, and then multiply by 5/9 or .5555.

To Convert C to F:
Multiply by 1.8
and then add 32.

32F = 0C

LIQUID VOLUME

To Convert:..................Multiply by
U.S. Gallons to Liters................ 3.8
U.S. Liters to Gallons 26
Imperial Gallons to U.S. Gallons 1.2
Imperial Gallons to Liters....... 4.55
Liters to Imperial Gallons 22
1 Liter = .26 U.S. Gallon
1 U.S. Gallon = 3.8 Liters

DISTANCE

To convert ....Multiply by
Inches to Centimeters 2.54
Centimeters to Inches 39
Feet to Meters...................... .3
Meters to Feet 3.28
Yards to Meters 91
Meters to Yards 1.09
Miles to Kilometers 1.61
Kilometers to Miles............ .62
1 Mile = 1.6 km
1 km = .62 Miles

WEIGHT

1 Ounce = .28 Grams
1 Pound = .4555 Kilograms
1 Gram = .04 Ounce
1 Kilogram = 2.2 Pounds

>TOURIST

TRAVEL QUESTIONS

- Do you bring presents home to family or friends after a vacation?
- Do you get motion sick?
- Do you have a favorite billboard?
- Do you know what to do if there is a flat tire?
- Do you like a sun roof open?
- Do you like to eat in the car?
- Do you like to wear sun glasses in the car?
- Do you like toppings on your ice cream?
- Do you use public bathrooms?
- Did you bring your cell phone and does it have power?
- Do you have a form of identification with you?
- Have you ever been pulled over by a cop?
- Have you ever given money to a stranger on a road trip?
- Have you ever taken a road trip with animals?
- Have you ever went on a vacation alone?
- Have you ever run out of gas?

- If you could move to any place in the world, where would it be?
- If you could travel anywhere in the world, where would you travel?
- If you could travel in any vehicle, which one would it be?
- If you had three things to wish for from a magic genie, what would they be?
- If you have a driver's license, how many times did it take you to pass the test?
- What are you the most afraid of on vacation?
- What do you want to get away from the most when you are on vacation?
- What foods smells bad to you?
- What item do you bring on ever trip with you away from home?
- What makes you sleepy?
- What song would you love to hear on the radio when you're cruising on the highway?
- What travel job would you want the least?
- What will you miss most while you are away from home?
- What is something you always wanted to try?

>TOURIST

- What is the best road side attraction that you ever saw?
- What is the farthest distance you ever biked?
- What is the farthest distance you ever walked?
- What is the weirdest thing you needed to buy while on vacation?
- What is your favorite candy?
- What is your favorite color car?
- What is your favorite family vacation?
- What is your favorite food?
- What is your favorite gas station drink or food?
- What is your favorite license plate design?
- What is your favorite restaurant?
- What is your favorite smell?
- What is your favorite song?
- What is your favorite sound that nature makes?
- What is your favorite thing to bring home from a vacation?
- What is your favorite vacation with friends?
- What is your favorite way to relax?

- Where is the farthest place you ever traveled in a car?
- Where is the farthest place you ever went North, South, East and West?
- Where is your favorite place in the world?
- Who is your favorite singer?
- Who taught you how to drive?
- Who will you miss the most while you are away?
- Who if the first person you will contact when you get to your destination?
- Who brought you on your first vacation?
- Who likes to travel the most in your life?
- Would you rather be hot or cold?
- Would you rather drive above, below, or at the speed limited?
- Would you rather drive on a highway or a back road?
- Would you rather go on a train or a boat?
- Would you rather go to the beach or the woods?

>TOURIST

TRAVEL BUCKET LIST

1.

2.

3.

4.

5.

6.

7.

8.

9.

10.

>TOURIST

NOTES

Made in the USA
San Bernardino, CA
20 March 2019